PIANO SOLOS
for LENT

30 Contemplative Hymns & Classical Pieces

HAL•LEONARD®

7777 W. BLUEMOUND RD. P.O. BOX 13819
MILWAUKEE, WISCONSIN 53213

ISBN 978-1-4950-9719-5

In Australia Contact:
Hal Leonard Australia Pty. Ltd.
4 Lenara Court
Cheltenham, Victoria, 3192 Australia
Email: ausadmin@halleonard.au

Visit Hal Leonard Online at
www.halleonard.com

Contents

AGNUS DEI
from MASS IN G MAJOR
excerpt

By FRANZ SCHUBERT
1797–1828

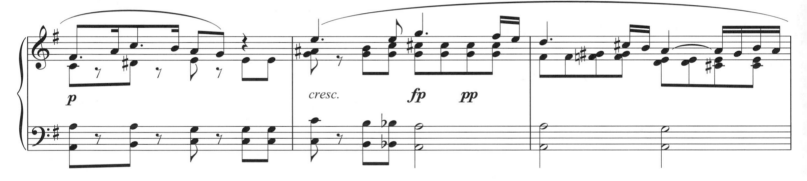

AH, HOLY JESUS

HERZLIEBSTER JESU

Words by JOHANN HEERMANN
Music by JOHANN CRÜGER

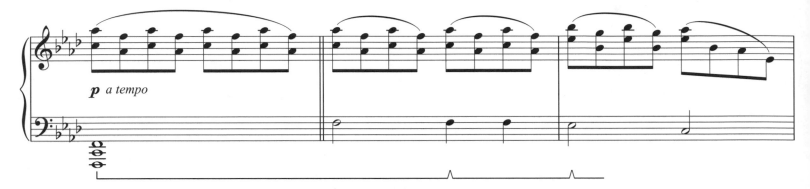

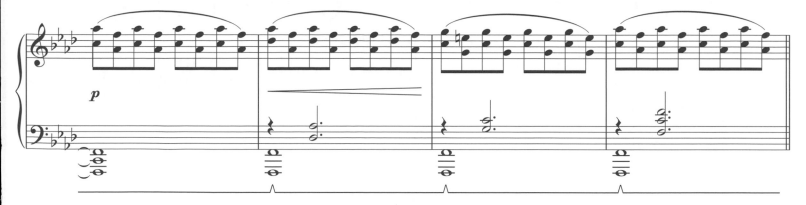

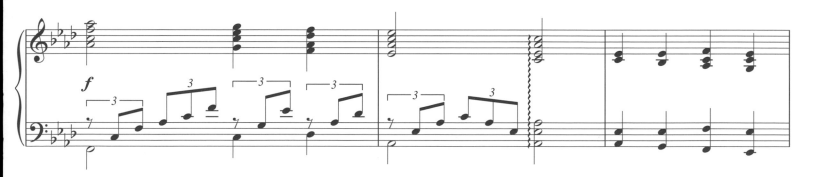

ALL GLORY, LAUD AND HONOR

VALET WILL ICH DIR GEBEN

Words by THEODULPH OF ORLEANS
Translated by JOHN MASON NEALE
Music by MELCHIOR TESCHNER

Majestically

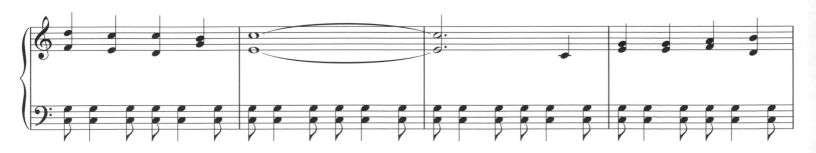

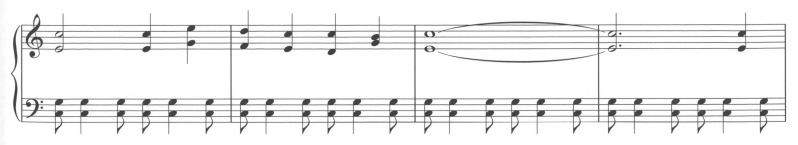

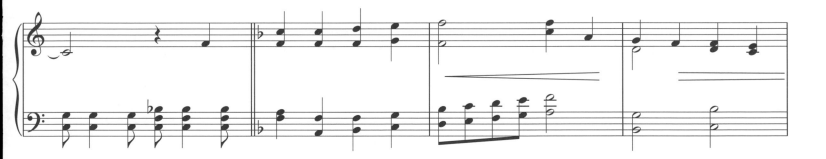

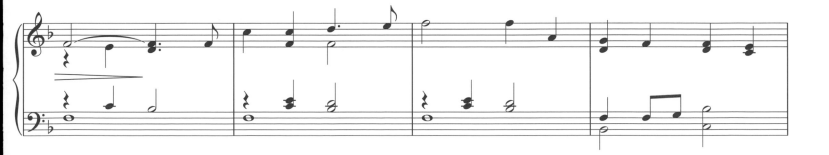

8vb

GO TO DARK GETHSEMANE

REDHEAD

Words by JAMES MONTGOMERY
Music by RICHARD REDHEAD

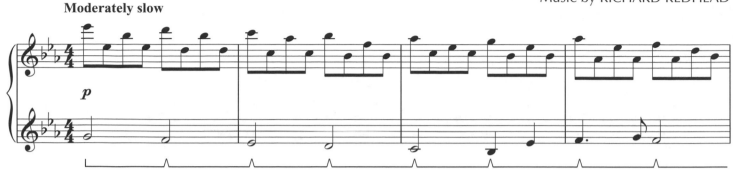

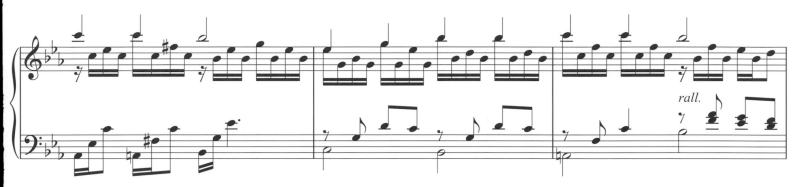

AVE VERUM CORPUS

By WOLFGANG AMADEUS MOZART
1756–1791
K. 618

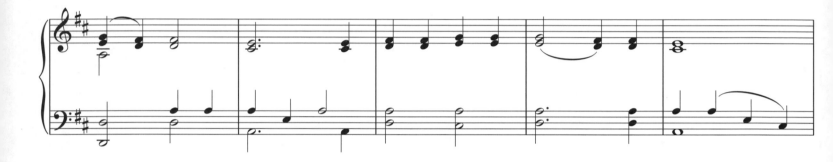

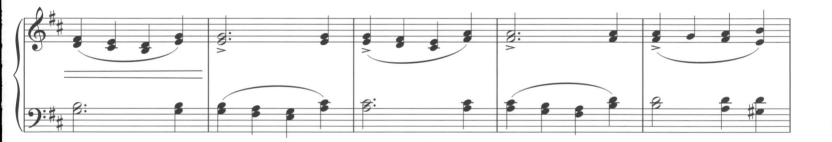

BE THOU MY VISION
SLANE

Traditional Irish

cresc.

mf

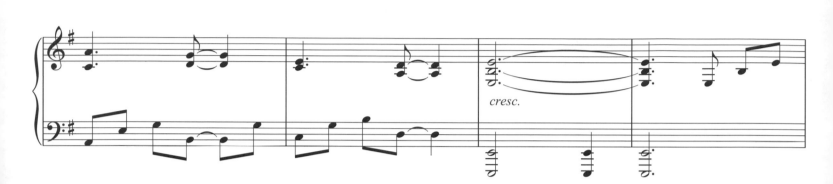

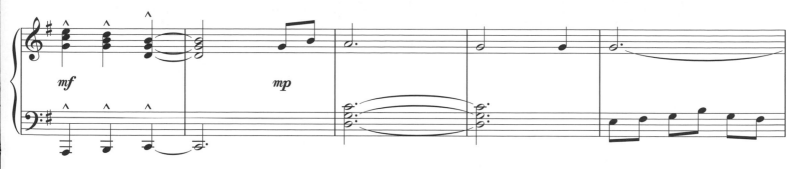

BENEATH THE CROSS OF JESUS
ST. CHRISTOPHER

Words by ELIZABETH CECELIA DOUGLAS CLEPHANE
Music by FREDERICK CHARLES MAKER

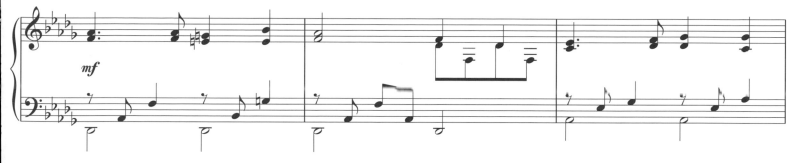

FORTY DAYS AND FORTY NIGHTS
AUS DER TIEFE RUFE ICH

Words by GEORGE H. SMYTTAN
and F. POTT
Music attributed to MARTIN HERBST

Flowing, not too fast

With pedal

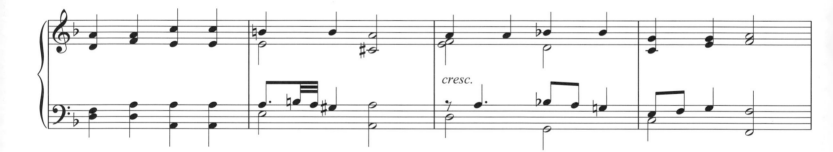

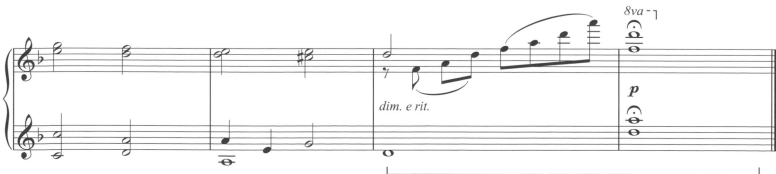

GOD SO LOVED THE WORLD

from the oratorio *The Crucifixion*

Words from John 3:16, 17
Music by JOHN STAINER

Slowly and solemnly

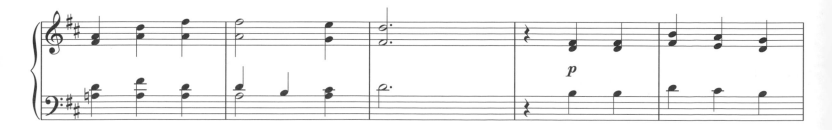

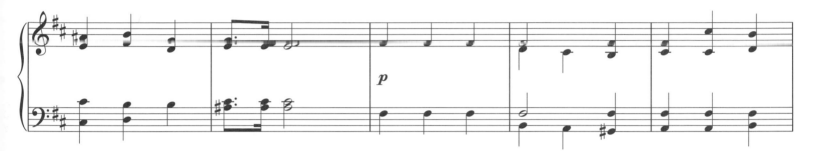

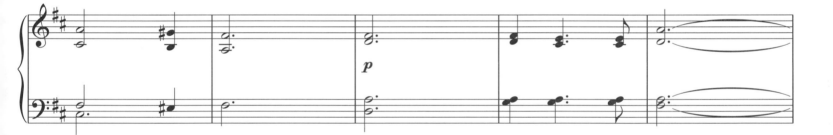

IN THE CROSS OF CHRIST I GLORY
RATHBUN

Words by JOHN BOWRING
Music by ITHAMAR CONKEY

Firmly, in Celtic style

HOSANNA, LOUD HOSANNA

ELLACOMBE

Words by JENETTE THRELFALL, based on Matthew 21:1-11
Music from *Gesangbuch der Herzogl*

JESUS, KEEP ME NEAR THE CROSS

NEAR THE CROSS

Words by FANNY J. CROSBY
Music by WILLIAM H. DOANE

Flowing, in one

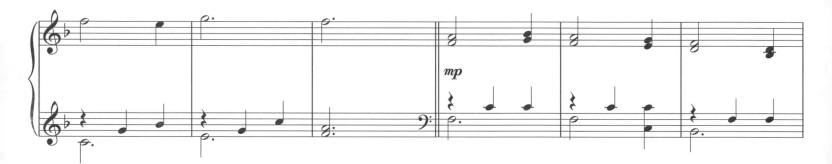

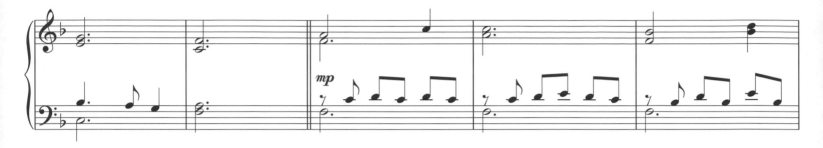

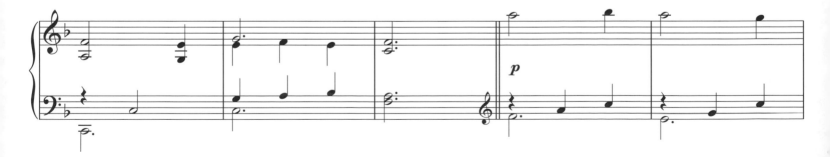

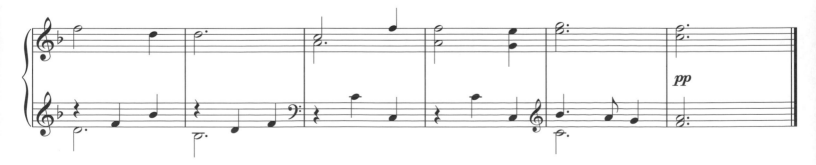

LORD, WHO THROUGHOUT THESE FORTY DAYS

ST. FLAVIAN

Words by CLAUDIA FRANCES HERNAMAN
Music from Day's *Psalter*

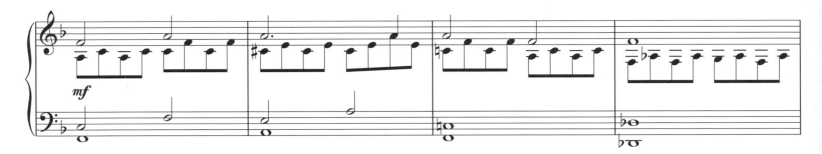

JESUS WALKED THIS LONESOME VALLEY

LONESOME VALLEY

Traditional Spiritual

Slow Gospel feeling

THE KING OF LOVE MY SHEPHERD IS

DOMINUS REGIT ME

Words by HENRY WILLIAM BAKER
Music by JOHN BACCHUS DYKES

Tenderly, not too fast

Meno mosso

MINUET
from WATER MUSIC

By GEORGE FRIDERIC HANDEL
1685–1759

Tempo di Minuetto

NEARER, MY GOD, TO THEE

BETHANY

Words by SARAH F. ADAMS
Based on Genesis 28:10–22
Music by LOWELL MASON

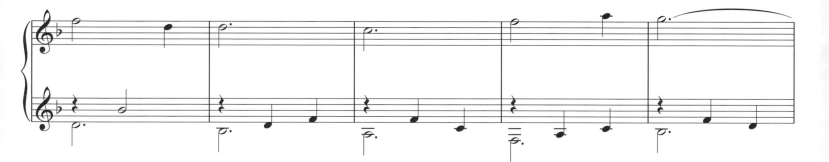

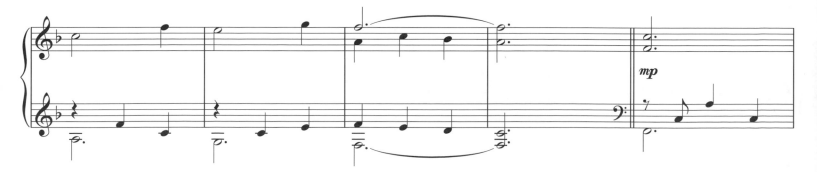

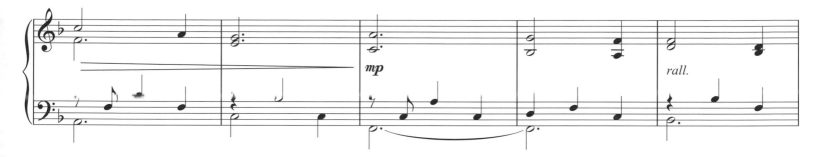

O LAMB OF GOD MOST HOLY
O LAMM GOTTES

Words and Music by NIKOLAUS DECIUS
Translated by ARTHUR TOZER RUSSELL

Flowing

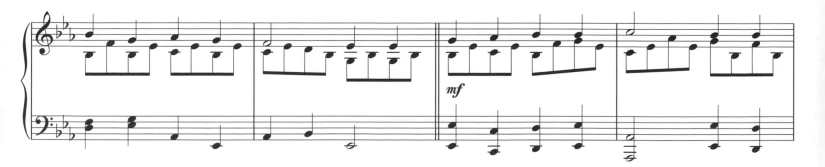

Più mosso

THE OLD RUGGED CROSS
OLD RUGGED CROSS

Words and Music by
REV. GEORGE BENNARD

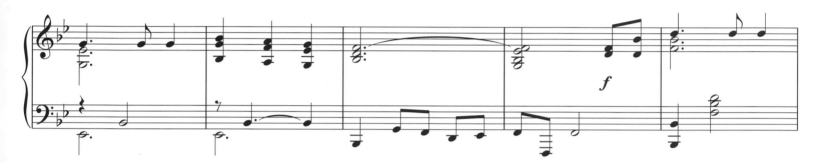

O SACRED HEAD, NOW WOUNDED

PASSION CHORALE

Words by BERNARD OF CLAIRVAUX
Music by HANS HASSLER

PANIS ANGELICUS
(O Lord Most Holy)

By CÉSAR FRANCK
1822–1890

Poco lento

With pedal

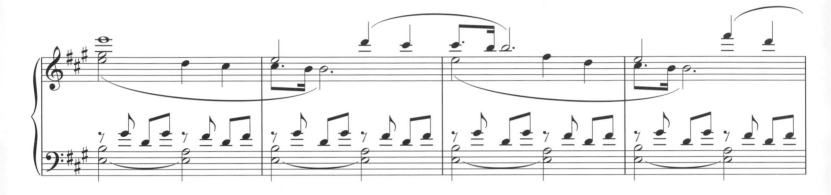

WHAT WONDROUS LOVE IS THIS
WONDROUS LOVE

American Folk Hymn
Music from William Walker's *Southern Harmony*

Gently flowing

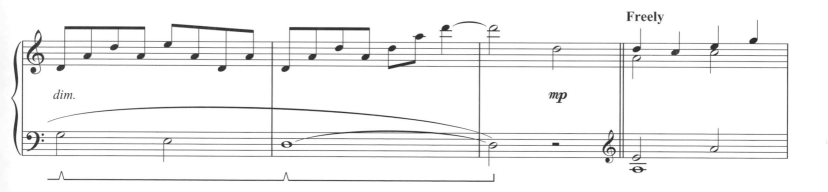

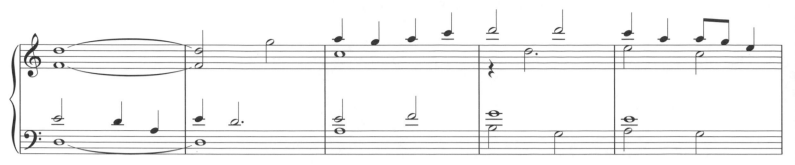

Gently flowing

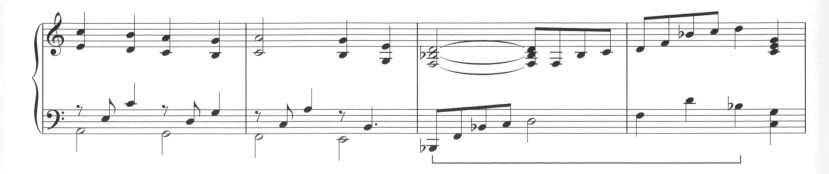

PIE JESU
from REQUIEM, Op. 48

By GABRIEL FAURÉ
1845–1924

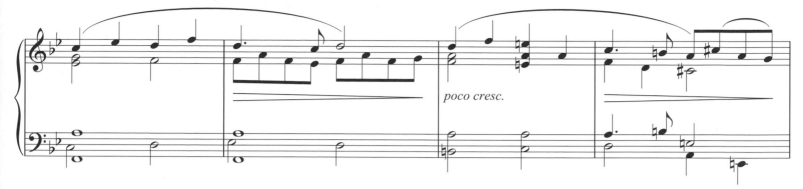

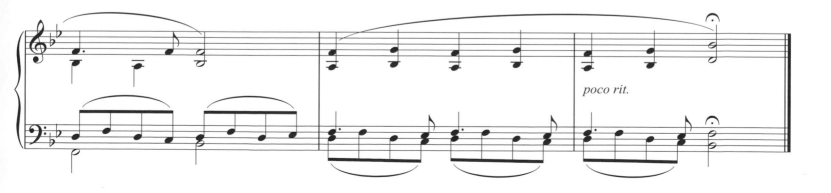

RIDE ON, KING JESUS

RIDE ON, KING JESUS

African-American Spiritual

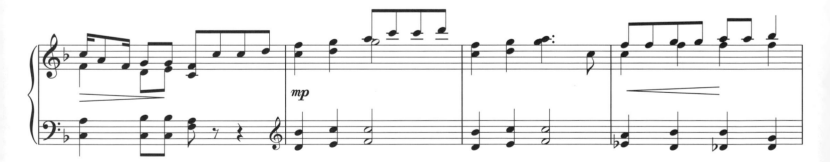

RIDE ON! RIDE ON IN MAJESTY!

ST. DROSTANE

Words by HENRY HART MILMAN
Music by JOHN BACCHUS DYKES

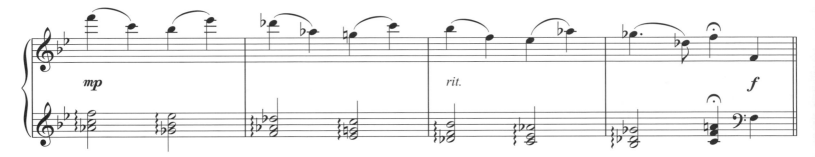

SICILIANO
from FLUTE SONATA IN E-FLAT MAJOR

By JOHANN SEBASTIAN BACH
1685–1750
BWV 1031

Moderately

SING, MY TONGUE, THE GLORIOUS BATTLE
PANGE LINGUA

Words by VENANTIUS HONORIUS FORTUNATUS
Translated by JOHN MASON NEALE
14th Century Plainsong

Meno mosso

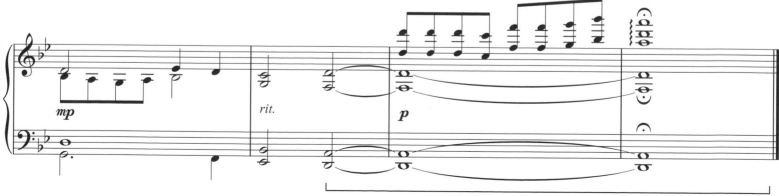

THOU SHALT BRING THEM IN

from ISRAEL IN EGYPT

By GEORGE FRIDERIC HANDEL
1685–1759

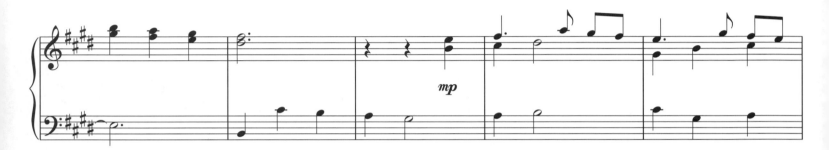

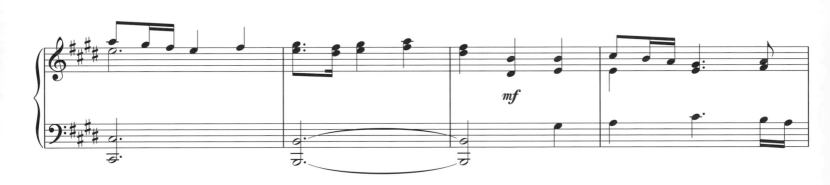

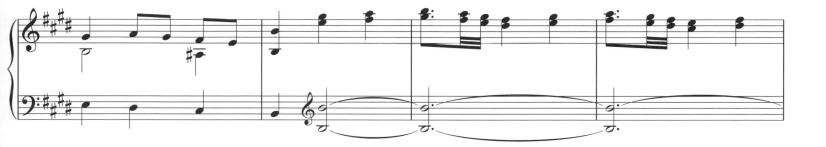

WERE YOU THERE?

WERE YOU THERE

African-American Spiritual

Slowly and reflectively

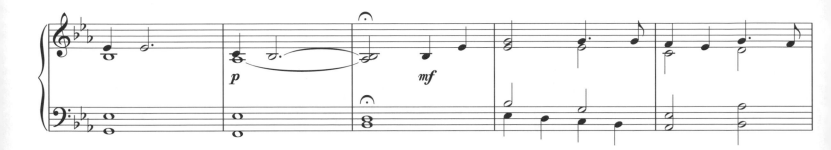

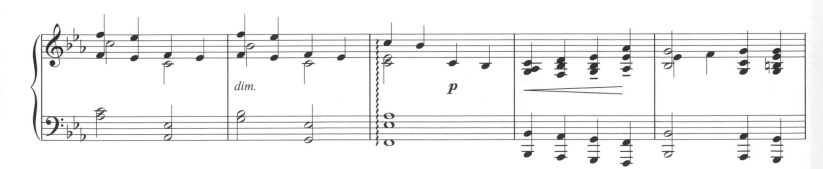

WHEN I SURVEY
THE WONDROUS CROSS

HAMBURG

Words by ISAAC WATTS
Music arranged by LOWELL MASON
Based on Plainsong

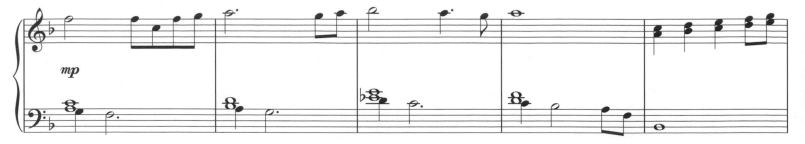

The Best
Sacred Collections
for Piano

Blended Worship Piano Collection

Songs include: Amazing Grace (My Chains Are Gone) • Be Thou My Vision • I Will Rise • Joyful, Joyful, We Adore Thee • Lamb of God • Majesty • Open the Eyes of My Heart • Praise to the Lord, the Almighty • Shout to the Lord • 10,000 Reasons (Bless the Lord) • Worthy Is the Lamb • Your Name • and more.
00293528 Piano Solo $17.99

Hymn Anthology

A beautiful collection of 60 hymns arranged for piano solo, including: Abide with Me • Be Thou My Vision • Come, Thou Fount of Every Blessing • Doxology • For the Beauty of the Earth • God of Grace and God of Glory • Holy, Holy, Holy • It Is Well with My Soul • Joyful, Joyful, We Adore Thee • Let Us Break Bread Together • A Mighty Fortress Is Our God • O God, Our Help in Ages Past • Savior, like a Shepherd Lead Us • To God Be the Glory • What a Friend We Have in Jesus • and more.
00251244 Piano Solo $16.99

The Hymn Collection
arranged by Phillip Keveren

17 beloved hymns expertly and beautifully arranged for solo piano by Phillip Keveren. Includes: All Hail the Power of Jesus' Name • I Love to Tell the Story • I Surrender All • I've Got Peace Like a River • Were You There? • and more.
00311071 Piano Solo $14.99

Hymn Duets
arranged by Phillip Keveren

Includes lovely duet arrangements of: All Creatures of Our God and King • I Surrender All • It Is Well with My Soul • O Sacred Head, Now Wounded • Praise to the Lord, The Almighty • Rejoice, The Lord Is King • and more.
00311544 Piano Duet..............................$14.99

Hymn Medleys
arranged by Phillip Keveren

Great medleys resonate with the human spirit, as do the truths in these moving hymns. Here Phillip Keveren combines 24 timeless favorites into eight lovely medleys for solo piano.
00311349 Piano Solo $14.99

P/V/G = Piano/Vocal/Guitar arrangements.

Prices, contents and availability subject to change without notice.

Hymns for Two
arranged by Carol Klose

12 piano duet arrangements of favorite hymns: Amazing Grace • Be Thou My Vision • Crown Him with Many Crowns • Fairest Lord Jesus • Holy, Holy, Holy • I Need Thee Every Hour • O Worship the King • What a Friend We Have in Jesus • and more.
00290544 Piano Duet..............................$12.99

It Is Well
10 BELOVED HYMNS FOR MEMORIAL SERVICES
arr. John Purifoy

10 peaceful, soul-stirring hymn settings appropriate for memorial services and general worship use. Titles include: Abide with Me • Amazing Grace • Be Still My Soul • For All the Saints • His Eye Is on the Sparrow • In the Garden • It Is Well with My Soul • Like a River Glorious • Rock of Ages • What a Friend We Have in Jesus.
00118920 Piano Solo $12.99

Ragtime Gospel Classics
arr. Steven K. Tedesco

A dozen old-time gospel favorites: Because He Lives • Goodbye World Goodbye • He Touched Me • I Saw the Light • I'll Fly Away • Keep on the Firing Line • Mansion over the Hilltop • No One Ever Cared for Me like Jesus • There Will Be Peace in the Valley for Me • Victory in Jesus • What a Day That Will Be • Where Could I Go.
00142449 Piano Solo $11.99

Ragtime Gospel Hymns
arranged by Steven Tedesco

15 traditional gospel hymns, including: At Calvary • Footsteps of Jesus • Just a Closer Walk with Thee • Leaning on the Everlasting Arms • What a Friend We Have in Jesus • When We All Get to Heaven • and more.
00311763 Piano Solo $10.99

Sacred Classics for Solo Piano
arr. John Purifoy

10 timeless songs of faith, masterfully arranged by John Purifoy. Because He Lives • Easter Song • Glorify Thy Name • Here Am I, Send Me • I'd Rather Have Jesus • Majesty • On Eagle's Wings • There's Something About That Name • We Shall Behold Him • Worthy Is the Lamb.
00141703 Piano Solo $14.99

Raise Your Hands
PIANO SOLOS FOR BLENDED WORSHIP
arr. Heather Sorenson

10 uplifting and worshipful solos crafted by Heather Sorenson. Come Thou Fount, Come Thou King • God of Heaven • Holy Is the Lord (with "Holy, Holy, Holy") • Holy Spirit • I Will Rise • In Christ Alone • Raise Your Hands • Revelation Song • 10,000 Reasons (Bless the Lord) • Your Name (with "All Hail the Power of Jesus' Name").
00231579 Piano Solo $14.99

Seasonal Sunday Solos for Piano

24 blended selections grouped by occasion. Includes: Breath of Heaven (Mary's Song) • Come, Ye Thankful People, Come • Do You Hear What I Hear • God of Our Fathers • In the Name of the Lord • Mary, Did You Know? • Mighty to Save • Spirit of the Living God • The Wonderful Cross • and more.
00311971 Piano Solo $16.99

Sunday Solos for Piano

30 blended selections, perfect for the church pianist. Songs include: All Hail the Power of Jesus' Name • Be Thou My Vision • Great Is the Lord • Here I Am to Worship • Majesty • Open the Eyes of My Heart • and many more.
00311272 Piano Solo $17.99

More Sunday Solos for Piano

A follow-up to *Sunday Solos for Piano*, this collection features 30 more blended selections perfect for the church pianist. Includes: Agnus Dei • Come, Thou Fount of Every Blessing • The Heart of Worship • How Great Thou Art • Immortal, Invisible • O Worship the King • Shout to the Lord • Thy Word • We Fall Down • and more.
00311864 Piano Solo $16.99

Even More Sunday Solos for Piano

30 blended selections, including: Ancient Words • Brethren, We Have Met to Worship • How Great Is Our God • Lead On, O King Eternal • Offering • Savior, Like a Shepherd Lead Us • We Bow Down • Worthy of Worship • and more.
00312098 Piano Solo $16.99

www.halleonard.com

Creative PIANO SOLO

Looking to add some variety to your playing? Enjoy these beautifully distinctive arrangements for piano solo! These popular tunes get new and unique treatments for a fun and fresh presentation. Explore new styles and enjoy these favorites with a bit of a twist! Each collection includes 20 songs for the intermediate to advanced player.

BOHEMIAN RHAPSODY & OTHER EPIC SONGS

Band on the Run • A Day in the Life • Free Bird • November Rain • Piano Man • Roundabout • Stairway to Heaven • Take the Long Way Home • and more.

00196019 Piano Solo......................................$14.99

CHRISTMAS CAROLS

Away in a Manger • Deck the Hall • The First Noel • God Rest Ye Merry, Gentlemen • Hark! the Herald Angels Sing • It Came upon the Midnight Clear • Jingle Bells • Joy to the World • O Holy Night • Silent Night • Up on the Housetop • We Three Kings of Orient Are • What Child Is This? • and more.

00147214 Piano Solo......................................$14.99

CHRISTMAS COLLECTION

Blue Christmas • The Christmas Song (Chestnuts Roasting on an Open Fire) • Frosty the Snow Man • Here Comes Santa Claus (Right down Santa Claus Lane) • Let It Snow! Let It Snow! Let It Snow! • Silver Bells • Sleigh Ride • White Christmas • Winter Wonderland • and more.

00172042 Piano Solo......................................$14.99

CLASSIC ROCK

Another One Bites the Dust • Aqualung • Beast of Burden • Born to Be Wild • Carry on Wayward Son • Layla • Owner of a Lonely Heart • Roxanne • Smoke on the Water • Sweet Emotion • Takin' It to the Streets • 25 or 6 to 4 • Welcome to the Jungle • and more!

00138517 Piano Solo......................................$14.99

Prices, contents, and availability subject to change without notice.

DISNEY FAVORITES

Beauty and the Beast • Can You Feel the Love Tonight • Chim Chim Cher-ee • For the First Time in Forever • How Far I'll Go • Let It Go • Mickey Mouse March • Remember Me (Ernesto de la Cruz) • You'll Be in My Heart • You've Got a Friend in Me • and more.

00283318 Piano Solo......................................$14.99

JAZZ POP SONGS

Don't Know Why • I Just Called to Say I Love You • I Put a Spell on You • Just the Way You Are • Killing Me Softly with His Song • Mack the Knife • Michelle • Smooth Operator • Sunny • Take Five • What a Wonderful World • and more.

00195426 Piano Solo......................................$14.99

JAZZ STANDARDS

All the Things You Are • Beyond the Sea • Georgia on My Mind • In the Wee Small Hours of the Morning • The Lady Is a Tramp • Like Someone in Love • A Nightingale Sang in Berkeley Square • Someone to Watch Over Me • That's All • What'll I Do? • and more.

00283317 Piano Solo......................................$14.99

POP BALLADS

Against All Odds (Take a Look at Me Now) • Bridge over Troubled Water • Fields of Gold • Hello • I Want to Know What Love Is • Imagine • In Your Eyes • Let It Be • She's Got a Way • Total Eclipse of the Heart • You Are So Beautiful • Your Song • and more.

00195425 Piano Solo......................................$14.99

POP HITS

Billie Jean • Fields of Gold • Get Lucky • Happy • Ho Hey • I'm Yours • Just the Way You Are • Let It Go • Poker Face • Radioactive • Roar • Rolling in the Deep • Royals • Smells like Teen Spirit • Viva la Vida • Wonderwall • and more.

00138156 Piano Solo......................................$14.99

HAL•LEONARD®
www.halleonard.com